FALLING CARS AND JUNKYARD DOGS

PORTRAITS FROM A MUSICAL LIFE

FALLING CARS AND JUNKYARD DOGS

JAY FARRAR

 SOFT SKULL PRESS · BERKELEY | AN IMPRINT OF COUNTERPOINT

Falling Cars and Junkyard Dogs: A Portrait of Musical Life
Copyright © 2013 Jay Farrar

Library of Congress Cataloging-in-Publication Data

Farrar, Jay.
Falling cars and junkyard dogs : a portrait of musical life / Jay Farrar.
    pages cm
ISBN 978-1-59376-512-5 (pbk.)
1. Farrar, Jay. 2. Alternative country musicians--United States--Biography.
I. Title.
ML420.F273A3 2013
782.42166092--dc23
[B]

2012046144

Cover design by Debbie Berne
Interior design by Elyse Strongin, Neuwirth & Associates, Inc.
All photographs courtesy of Jay Farrar

Soft Skull Press
An Imprint of Counterpoint
1919 Fifth Street
Berkeley, CA 94710

www.softskull.com
Distributed by Publishers Group West
Printed in the United States of America

10 9 8 7 6 5 4 3 2 1

To Monica and Mother D for making the world go around.

———————————

Special thanks to Jane Ganahl, Charlie Winton, Kelly Winton, Barrett Briske, and Susan Clements.

CONTENTS

6

FALLING CARS AND JUNKYARD DOGS

1

Ozarks

MAR 1954

AUX ARC REDS

guess you could say I had Ozark Commie parents, at least that's the way my dad tells the story.

"I returned to Potosi, Missouri, in 1957, on leave from the Merchant Marine. I was just hanging out with nothing to do when someone suggested I should meet a new teacher at the high school who was causing a stir by standing up for communism, so I asked a friend to introduce me to this communist sympathizer, and we hooked up after that."

Of course neither of my parents were really communists; this was the McCarthy era after all. Extolling any virtue of communism couldn't go unnoticed, especially out in the hills of Washington County, Missouri.

The political beliefs of my father could probably best be described as Libertarian . . . where the far right meets the left and the far left meets the right. It was a murky political landscape around my father, whereas my mother—with a four-year college degree and a teaching job—fell more in line with the collegiate worldview of the times. These two alternately copacetic and conflicting ideologies played out in interesting ways.

"We were married about six years when we realized we had fundamentally differing views and allegiances when it came to discussing the Civil War," said my mother. "We almost divorced over it." So the residual dichotomy of the American Civil War conflict manifested in my childhood family dynamic. In retrospect, I see it all clearly now.

One of my earliest childhood memories of my mom is of walking into her bedroom and seeing her standing on her head. She was into yoga and the good earth, and her guru was a guy named Euell Gibbons who wrote a book on horticulture. Once as punishment for taking a hatchet to a tree, my brothers and I had to read the chapters of Euell's book that explained how to concoct natural salves and medicines and apply them to the tree wound—which we did.

Contrast that with memories of one of my father's hobbies—basically stabbing at moles with a Spanish American War–era cavalry sword. Since "Stabbing the Mole" involved smoking tobacco and drinking coffee, my father would do it for hours on end, sitting silently on a stool with sword in hand, waiting for the mole to make a subterranean move. He was contemplative—yet ready to kill. Occasionally he got the mole. Ultimately though, the payoff was simple. Quiet time with old friends: coffee and cigarettes.

VELMA

Velma smoked a lot and lived in a trailer. Velma also disliked kids. This predilection and aversion presented a problem for me when I was kid and Velma was my paternal grandmother. Velma's three sons (my father and uncles) would stop by to visit Velma for half-day coffee-and-cigarette sessions, so my brothers and I would often go along to see grandma.

"Seeing" grandma meant venturing into the trailer where she sat in an easy chair while a thick smoky haze blanketed all available breathable airspace except for one foot of clear air at floor level. This untenable circumstance would last until we boys would start coughing and laughing at the absurdity of all the smoke. Velma would thereby tell us to "get out"—to her way of thinking, cigarettes were sacrosanct and laughing at smoke was not.

Getting yelled at by grandma was good for brotherly camaraderie, but we were forever thereafter on the bad side of Velma. We didn't know of the hardship Velma had faced as a fifteen-year-old mother who eventually raised six boys and a girl during the Depression in a remote hollow of the southern Ozarks that she dubbed "Lost Vegas."

Velma's funeral was held in the Ozarks, and after her casket was in the ground, those folks who had come to pay their respects piled into cars and formed a caravan with destination unknown. (My immediate family and I were the "city folks," and we didn't know where we were going or what was about to happen.) The post-funeral procession drove for a few miles and then pulled into an empty field. Before the engines were off and the dust had settled, the banjos and guitars were out and the post-funeral bluegrass celebration was full on . . .

DESICCANT

"Jim! Jim! What are you doing?" screamed Chun Ae. "Very good, delicious Jim . . . no!"

"Well now honey, you're not supposed to eat it—these packets keep the candy dry," replied my father, as he threw the packets in the trash bin.

The year was 1952, and James Farrar had been drafted at the age of twenty-two into the U. S. Army and was stationed at Inchon, South Korea, for the duration of the conflict. My father kept a black-and-white photo of his girlfriend Chun Ae in his wallet—he said he almost married her but instead returned from the conflict to his hometown of Potosi, Missouri, and married the local high school English teacher (my mother).

Before meeting my mother in 1957, however, my father signed up for a two-year expedition to the South Pole. Many of my childhood years were spent as a captive audience to 8 mm movies of the South Pole expedition, wherein narrative stories of penguins, seals, and the finding of Ernest Shackleton's outpost on the mainland were the order of the day. He brought back souvenirs from Shackleton's hut, like hinges and doorknobs. This stuff didn't resonate till years later when I read about Shackleton's adventures and learned of the resilient perseverance and quixotic hardships Shackleton engaged in and endured.

As a kid what I found most curious and odd about my father was his method of working on old cars while resting on his haunches. My brothers and I all tried it and laughed when we fell backwards, as we were unable to do what our aging father did effortlessly. He had learned the stance from Korean mechanics during his stay at Inchon.

A successful cultural exchange, I'd say, in the midst of all the bloodshed, in the form of a beautiful woman wearing a Kimono in a faded photograph and a man resting on his haunches, at peace with the world.

BREACH OF PROMISE

The first "breach of promise" lawsuit of the new world was brought about in 1622 by a Rev. Greville Pooley, who made the assertion that any consent of marriage between my ancestors, William Farrar and Cicely Jordan, should be considered invalid.

Cicely was born in England around the year 1600, presumably as an orphan, and immigrated to Jamestown, Virginia, on a ship called *The Swan* in 1610. The early arrival of Cicely to Virginia made her one of the first European women to reach the new world, and the resultant reality of supply and demand would factor prominently in later events that shaped her life.

William Farrar left out of London and arrived in Virginia in 1619 aboard a ship called *Neptune*. William was an investor in the third charter of the Virginia Company of London, which had established a colony in 1611 called "Citie of Henrico," which later came to be known as Farrar's Island.

The paths of Cicely Jordan and William Farrar would coalesce in 1622 as a result of a Native American attack on the English colonist settlements. William Farrar escaped the assault and took refuge at the better-fortified plantation of Cicely Jordan and her husband Samuel, which was known as "Jordan's Journey." Samuel Jordan died a year after the Native American attack in 1623. With the death of Samuel Jordan, Cicely was now twenty-three years of age, pregnant, and un-married, in a settlement with a dearth of eligible females. The competition for her hand in marriage was immediate. Rev. Greville Pooley performed the funeral rites for her husband while subsequently proposing marriage within a span of hours.

Rev. Pooley attempted to marry Cicely without her consent by reciting the words of a marriage service—speaking the words for her as well as for himself.

Cicely, however, accepted her other suitor, William Farrar, instead. Consequently, Reverend Pooley took the matter to court, but the court referred the case to the Virginia Company of London, which punted the case back to the court. Eventually, after several years, Rev. Pooley withdrew the breach-of-promise suit, and the marriage of William Farrar and Cicely Jordan was formally allowed and accepted in Virginia. Three hundred and eighty-four years later, this was all news to me.

THE LAST BATTLE

The American Civil War was still going on in the twentieth century. The issue at hand that caused what was perhaps the last battle of the American Civil War was: what to name me on the day I was born. As a result of these hostilities over naming rights, I was at the hospital for the first day of my life without a name.

Negotiations between the North (my mother) and the South (my father) continued while I tried to make sense of the transition from the warmth of the womb to being nameless in the stark environs of a hospital. History has a way of repeating itself, and once again, the South lost the last battle. As it turned out, I was not named "Stonewall" (Stonewall Jackson) or "Jubal" (Jubal Early) or Jeb (J.E.B. Stuart) or "Forrest" (Nathan Bedford Forrest), as these Confederate general names were preferentially presented by the South—but summarily dismissed by the North.

Thanks, Ma . . .

2

Illinois

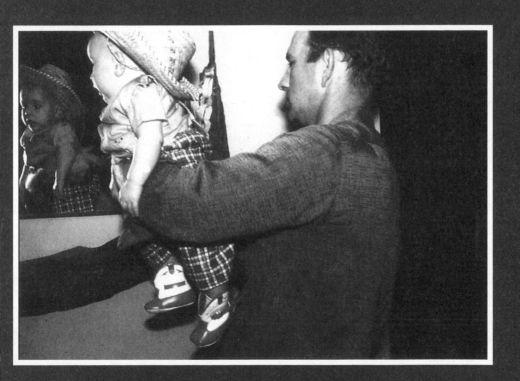

CHAIN SAW MORNING

I t was a day etched in memory . . . he seemed agitated and somewhat possessed, so we kept our distance. I was around ten years old and my three brothers were older. We stood bemused as our father took a chain saw to a freestanding upright old log. It was understood that he wouldn't hurt us, but we weren't sure he wouldn't manage to hurt himself.

The jarring sounds of the chainsaw continued for hours—the staccato growl gradually segued into the whine of an electric drill. The drill was for the detail work. When he finished later that day, we were astounded. A three-foot-high wooden sculpture of our father in a Civil War uniform was not what we had expected at all.

"How did you know it was going to look like you?"

"I didn't."

The sculpture became the family lawn ornament for the better part of ten years, till the termites had their say and took it down for good.

TAPS

ead dogs, dead cats, dead rabbits, dead turtles . . . it didn't matter that that none of them originated from a pet store. They were family pets—so when they died they were all given a military-style funeral and burial. My father had somehow procured an old cavalry bugle for these affairs. He would play "Taps" on the bugle while we kids gave our best ceremonial salutes . . .

EAST ST. LOUIS

East St. Louis is where I lived until I was four years of age. I had no knowledge of the race riots that occurred in 1917, nor was I aware of the white exodus of the 1960s. I was there until 1970, and the music that filtered down from my three older brothers was real good—James Brown, Joe Tex, and The Jackson 5. The most lasting memory-related association that I still have with East St. Louis is of my dad and brothers and me taking pieces of cardboard and sliding down a steep ravine of frosty frozen mud (there was no snow) to a creek-bed bottom below. This East St. Louisan was laughing all the way down . . .

CAHOKIANS

As a kid I remember thinking it strange that there was a large Indian mound on one side of the street and a Grandpa Pidgeon's on the other. Grandpa Pidgeon's was like a precursor to Walmart, where one could get anything from guns to clothes to musical instruments. I spent a lot of time perusing the Harmony and Japanese guitars for sale in the instrument aisle. A short distance away was "Monks Mound," which is the largest in a group of mounds (one square mile in diameter) built by the Mississippian culture, which disappeared except for the mounds that have survived the elements and waves of "new world" settlers. Monks Mound sits adjacent to Interstate 70, and hulking even more impressively ominous on the other side of the interstate is a massive earth-covered mound replete with vertical pipes spouting flames (burning off methane gas) and the constant activity of bulldozers and scavenger birds. This mound was built by the twentieth- and twenty-first-century American culture, which is not yet extinct . . .

ACROSS THE STREET

Daniel Ashbury and I used to wave at each other from our respective sides of the street. Sometimes Daniel wouldn't wave, so we would just look at each other for a while and then move on to something else. The street between us was recessed with up to twenty-foot embankments on both sides—ostensibly perfect for playing with the same-aged boy across the street, to my six-year-old way of thinking.

"Why can't I go play with Daniel?" "You can't. It's not safe."

At school I got to know Daniel enough to consider him a friend, but Daniel was rarely in class, and before the school year was over, Daniel was dead. Remembering the circumstances of Daniel's death is like peeling the scab off of a wound. Time heals, but there is a scar to mark the time and place.

Several months before Daniel was found dead, I was awakened by the commotion of voices and flashing lights. The police were at my house. It was around midnight in the early spring—when the weather is cold—when Daniel showed up at my house, half-naked and shivering with feces smeared in his eyes, his mouth, and around his wrists, asking for food and water. Daniel had told neighbors and teachers at school that he was kept in a cage-like cell at home and was abused by his stepmother. Already by the age of six, Daniel had multiple metal plates inserted in his skull from an unexplained bathtub incident that also left him with second-degree burns.

It was difficult for the mind of a six-year-old first grader to comprehend the cruelty and inhumanity that Daniel Ashbury suffered. Now, thirty-six years later, it's still starkly incomprehensible. They told me he had died after spending the night in a car with no water.

The cause of death was from ingestion of anti-freeze that had been put into a Coca-Cola container and left in the car. Daniel was taken to a hospital, where it took him fourteen hours to die. Maybe he made a decision to drink the poison in a Coke bottle to be free from purgatory . . . only Daniel knows hell and the reason.

THIRTEEN CARS

"Take out the trash when you get home from school."

"Okay, Pop."

As a kid, taking out the trash meant hefting it several hundred yards to the rear of the family property and then burning the garbage in an old oil drum, the same way "Rocky" and his pals would gather round to sing doo-wop and keep their hands warm. No singing around the fire for me, though there was a cavalier interest in throwing objects into the barrel that might explode (batteries, light bulbs). A lot of acrid fumes from plastics and Styrofoam to ponder—I guess that was my shared experience with kids from third-world countries.

High school was the age when I began to realize that not everyone had a hillbilly father who harbored thirteen cars in various stages of assembly, five motorcycles, and one wooden self-depiction sculpture cut with a chainsaw. Pop was born in 1930, at the front end of the Great Depression, and the first ten years of his life were spent in that era. Poverty? I asked my mother once why Pop always slept on a couch and not a bed. She explained that he was never comfortable on a bed because he didn't have one as a kid. This observation bears truth because Pop exclusively slept on a couch ("devonette" as he called it) after my folks divorced.

The second great depression for my father was an unfortunate but inevitable convergence of circumstances that resulted in the destruction of two of his most valued cars (a 1956 MG convertible and a 1958 Sunbeam convertible), all of the motorcycles (a Sears BMW, a Cushman three-wheel, and a Cushman two-wheel), as well as my ride at the time (an early '60s Honda 50). High winds took burning embers from the ritualistic oil-drum garbage fire to nearby fallen tree leaves that had collected around the barn where the vintage cars and motorcycles were stored, resulting in fire and devastation. After the fire, Pop sunk into a general depressed state that lasted many years till, ironically, he was diagnosed with terminal cancer. The diagnosis spurred an epiphany, and Pop lived a renaissance of sorts through his remaining years.

As for me, I had a few years to go in high school with no motorbike, but the upside was that thereafter, for ten dollars a month, the Belleville Township Waste Disposal trucks picked up the garbage just a few steps away. In the end, despite a classic car and motorbike defeat, no more toxic smoke from the backyard incinerator seemed a clear environmental victory . . .

MELTING POT

To this day I am perplexed as to why I can hum the melody and approximate the words to several Hebrew folk songs.

Although my father encouraged me to play guitar as a toddler, the task of giving guitar lessons was undertaken by my mother. While other kids out there were learning from Mel Bay books, I was being taught from the Laura Weber folk song book. "Hava Nagila" had the minor chords and quirky gypsy rhythms that resonated with me more than the somewhat tired Americana folk songs like "Down in the Valley" or "On Top of Old Smokey."

The initiation into the charms of the melting-pot song "Hava Nagila" led to my brother Wade and me walking around the house singing the Jewish hymn "Hine Ma Tov" from the movie *Raid on Entebbe* . . . Two little Middle Americans ready to join the Israeli Army . . .

PATTON

It was the only movie we went to see as a family, according to my mother. My father had the inspiration and rounded us up in the Ford Fairlane station wagon and took us to see the celluloid version of his hero Patton. The year was 1970, and I was four years old, with no prior briefing about "Old Blood and Guts," but Patton's penchant for profanity in the movie was no match for the major league curse words of my father.

The length of the movie was not a deterrent, as my mother said I stayed awake, transfixed. Fast forward to 1979, and I'm off to see a movie with my brother Wade (my third movie in a cinema—the second being *Star Wars*). We chose to see Monty Python's *Life of Brian*.

On the way out—while still whistling "Always Look on the Bright Side of Life"—we poked our heads into an adjacent cinema that was showing *Apocalypse Now*. We entered just as the boat was arriving at the camp of Colonel Kurtz in Cambodia. It was a dramatic shift from Monty Python that kept us riveted to the end. It wasn't until years later that I realized that the man responsible for two of the most influential movies of all time (and of my childhood) was Francis Ford Coppola. Thanks for the movies, Frank . . . The wine's good, but the movies are better . . .

LEAD CAR IN THE PARADE

Pop rarely picked me up from fifth-grade basketball practice—as he would be gone for three-month stretches, working as a boat engineer on a Mississippi River Corps of Engineers' dredge boat. Usually my mom picked me up in a 1970 Ford LTD station wagon—already on the old side in 1978, but a relatively "new" car in my experience.

Pop's style was to roll with a little more flair. His car du jour was a 1965 Ford Fairlane station wagon, treated with Pop's own rust-prevention technique: old rags soaked in liquid fiberglass and then applied to cover the plentiful proliferation of rust-hole wounds. This was instrumental in laying the foundation for the "clown pants for cars" look—though I think Pop's ethos leaned a lot more towards the "hippie pants for cars" look. To round out the aesthetic, there were hand-painted irregular racing stripes on the hood and sides with bonus self-adhesive bath-mat flowers to cover any defiant rust that wasn't already covered by fiberglass rags and racing stripes. Pop wasn't a hippie (no hair, no hippie), but when the bath-mat flowers went on the car, I knew something was up. Dread thereby entered the picture as I knew the fateful day would come when this glorious machine would be my ride home from basketball practice.

It was when the usual playground cacophony turned to dead silence that I knew I was done for. The moment I had expected and loathed had arrived. The silence morphed into a crowd of thirty or so kids screaming, laughing, pointing . . . A clown car had arrived to take away the drudgery and banality of Middle America elementary school life! I suppose it was a defining moment for me. I learned to go for the underdog and eschew the herd mentality of the mainstream.

Pop was a freethinker, and I have to thank him for teaching his brand of life lessons.

Oh yeah, while on the subject of life lessons, did I mention that Pop was an ex-merchant-marine sailor who, as an idiosyncratic form of meditation, could spew an endless profane diatribe at inanimate objects (i.e. engines)? "Why you motherfucking cocksucking good for nothing piece of shit . . . Goddamn you, you motherfucker . . . Jeeezuz fuckin' Christ . . . Gawwwwwd damn you cocksucker piece of shit motherfucker" . . . ad infinitum—with all words interchangeable and repeated for supreme efficacy. As a result, I savor the use of profanity like a French chef treats a truffle. I absorbed enough "motherfucker cocksucker shit" to last a lifetime.

3

Beat Bars and the Maritime

POPS FARRAR

My father was Beat. Not a literary Beat like Jack Kerouac or William Burroughs, but a Neal Cassady-esque hillbilly version from the Missouri Ozarks. He joined the Merchant Marine in 1947 at the age of seventeen and shipped out of New York City a few years after Woody Guthrie and a few years before Jack Kerouac. The interest of my father was not poems but the poetry of machinery. All things mechanized captured his interest—cars, motorcycles, boats, tractors—just about anything with an engine that would crank up and go. Like the Beats, my father traveled the globe as a merchant marine and fostered an appreciation of the diversity and wonder the world has to offer.

ENGINE MAN

He was an engine man—Briggs and Stratton, Tecumseh, V-8 Ford, and Wankel. Being an engine man meant he was impressed by speed. The publicity surrounding the success of the Mazda RX-7 as a racing car and the unorthodox Wankel rotary engine that it utilized was like a drug for my father. He bought the Wankel engine manuals, studied them, and gave household stump speeches about the superiority of the engine design. All of this behavior ultimately led to his purchase of a white Mazda RX-3 station wagon from Mudd Duck Salvage for $375. After copious amounts of nicotine and coffee consumed simultaneously along with inspired profanity salvos directed at the recalcitrant Wankel engine during the reconstruction process, the refurbished junkyard RX-3 station wagon was ready for action.

His face would enlighten and his tone and mannerisms would suddenly become animated as he recounted his favorite junkyard jewel success story. Interspersed throughout the telling of the story are the opposing car engine sounds of the protagonist (*eeeeraaaaavoom*) and the antagonist (*waaaaazeeeeeoooom*). I think for my father this story was symbolic of his ethos and personal disdain for the amount of money spent on a Corvette. Corvettes were the ubiquitous phallic-symbol fast cars of the day.

As the story goes, my father went to pass a Corvette, at which point the Corvette took offense and accelerated. Accordingly, my father's Mazda RX-3 junkyard station wagon with Wankel engine and manual transmission overtook the Corvette enough for my father to pass it and move to the right lane ahead of the Corvette. The Corvette driver then kicked into high gear and pulled alongside my father's car, projecting a glance of momentary confusion before pulling ahead and passing my father forever with a look of self-satisfaction.

It was the initial moment of exasperation on the Corvette driver's face that set the world right for my father. Not exactly a win, but a perennial source of inspiration for patriarchal junkyard aficionados the world over . . .

ROLL YOUR OWN

Even as a kid, I found it to be a fascinating ritual. Because of my father's six-foot-one-inch stature, his knees seemed to be proportioned just about right to get the job done while driving.

The usual routine did require a bit of slouching, though, to achieve optimal knee pressure. Without question, the first necessary piece of equipment was a plastic bag of Captain Black Pipe Tobacco. Next was a packet of TOP rolling papers. An optional instrument was the cigarette holder—which was actually a plastic disposable tar filter, but my father didn't care at all about tar. To be sure, Pops would use the same inexpensive plastic filter indefinitely until it was broken or lost, with any hope of tar reduction efficacy likely overloaded or spent in the first week.

With all ingredients and equipment in place now, the balancing act begins. Reduce speed by ten miles per hour. Both hands at this point are engaged and off the steering wheel. Maximum knee-driving has begun. Left and right hand together make a half-cylinder out of rolling paper. Ready to accept tobacco. Left hand holds aforementioned half cylinder of rolling paper while right hand unravels plastic Captain Black Tobacco bag and then grabs a large pinch between thumb and pointer finger. Left hand with rolling paper is now on reserve alert as a steering wheel guide in case of unforeseen potholes or other distractions. Knees are steady as she goes—still in control at the five o'clock and seven o'clock positions on the steering wheel.

A slight back-and-forth and left-to-right knee movement on the steering wheel maximizes stability and achieves optimal knee-steering directional calibration. The ratio of eyes-on-tobacco versus eyes-on-the-road is five to two—five seconds building cigarette with two-second glances at the road ahead. The tobacco level in paper half-cylinder is now on target. With the final adjustments by hand and mouth made to nascent cigarette, the car lighter is engaged. In less than five minutes, the entire process is done. Nicotine-delivery device is armed and ready for fire . . .

SOUTH POLE

Watching 8 mm home movies was a big deal. The TVs in my house were still black-and-white and Spartan in size in the 1970s, so watching my father's 8 mm films was a chance to watch something in color on a big screen with narration courtesy of my father.

"Here's where we were stuck in the ice for a few days," explained my father as images of dead bloody seals (to feed the dogs?) juxtaposed with footage of frolicsome penguins rolled across the screen. I guess being stuck in the ice was a good thing, as my father looked as jovial as the penguins when he appeared onscreen.

It was never clear what the purpose of the Navy expedition was that my father had signed up for. Maybe it was just to see what a bunch of guys will do when they get stuck in the ice for a few days. Thanks to 8 mm home movies . . . now we know.

LAISSEZ-FAIRE

"**W**hat are you doing, Pop?"

"I'm smoking a marijuana cigarette—I want to see what its effects are. That way I can tell you boys what to look out for."

I was about eleven years of age and incredulous both at the fact that my dad was openly smoking a joint and at the reality that he had traveled the world as a merchant sailor while also living through the 1960s and had never dabbled with reefer.

"It's really not as bad as alcohol, son—it makes you more careful." Under the effects of the THC, Pop became extremely safety-conscious.

"Where are you going with that BB gun?"

In retrospect, maybe a little more cannabis intake for Pop could have counteracted some of the laissez-faire Ozark culture of guns that he grew up with and subsequently passed down to me. By age twelve, I was allowed to shoot Pop's deceased Uncle Harry's ancient 22-caliber rifle. Any potential serious gun fascination for me ended abruptly during one episode when I was walking with two neighborhood boys (they had BB guns) through some nearby woods when the old 22 rifle spontaneously and randomly fired.

Fortunately—and to Pop's credit—he had instructed me in basic gun safety and the rifle barrel was pointed down when it misfired. The realization that I cold have hurt or killed one of my neighbor friends with an antiquated piece-of-junk rifle called for a reassessment and potential reversal of traditional father/son roles and all of the socioeconomic, generational, and cultural/geographic aspects involved.

The basic epiphany: Guns bad. Guitars good.

DREDGE BOATS

He retired at age fifty-five from working in the engine room of a dredge boat on the Mississippi River for the Army Corps of Engineers. Retirement for my father became a lost fifteen-year period of coffee, nicotine, and restlessness interspersed with a part-time job fixing "reefers," or refrigerated railroad cars, at the Alton and Southern railyard.

By the time he reached seventy years of age, he was diagnosed with terminal lung cancer (single cell carcinoma) from roll-your-own cigarettes and mesothelioma contracted from asbestos-filled engine rooms on boats. With this news, my father awoke from his fifteen-year retirement trance and began to fraternize with writers, artists, and musicians—mostly in the old Soulard section of St. Louis. Thus he made the rounds of communes, bar stages, and recording studios, stopped working on reefers and started smoking a different kind.

He stoically did all the chemotherapy to stay alive while eschewing the opiate pain pills till the very end of his days. The end completed a full circle—he went out the same way he came in—finding inspiration and solace in music and seeking camaraderie in others whose ethos echoed his own.

A few years after his passing, I came across these words from Woody Guthrie, which encapsulate a part of my father's lifelong inspiration and give meaning to the years of songs that he sang: "Music is the language of the mind that travels . . . it carries the key to the laws of time and space . . ."

BRASS BUCKLE

We talked about James B. Eads and all of his accomplishments, from the first bridge in the world constructed of steel to Civil War Ironclads to Eads's use of eddies and the power of the Mississippi river to cut it's own shipping channel. The next morning I found my father unconscious and having a seizure from the late-stage effects of cancer.

He had rolled to the floor, and his body was undulating silently where he lay. The image of the paramedics lifting my father's body up by grabbing the large belt buckle that he wore and using it as a hoist is seared into memory.

To the paramedics, using the buckle attached to his belt was a practical means to lift an unconscious, emaciated body. To my father, the belt buckle symbolized his heritage and defined his place in society.

The buckle was a large, brass, oval-shaped medallion that read "CSA" for Confederate States of America. The CSA belt buckle was the protagonist in one of my father's merchant sailor stories. "Cooky" (the name merchant sailors often gave to mess hall cooks) and my father got into an altercation involving a woman and two local men with knives in a bar in Hamburg, Germany. As the story goes, my father slipped off the CSA buckle and belt and used it as a deterrent to the knife-wielding locals—which facilitated the escape of Cooky and my father and ultimately allowed the birth of me.

Years later while touring the John Steinbeck museum in Salinas, California, one of Steinbeck's personal items on display caught my attention. It was identical. There it was: the large, brass, oval-shaped "Confederate States of America" belt buckle . . .

HANK WILLIAMS SR.

"I saw Hank Williams at an outdoor stage on the banks of Horseshoe Lake in Granite City, Illinois."

The year was about 1951, and Pops was twenty-one, back from the Merchant Marine and having a good time. "I shook his hand after the show," my father liked to point out.

Hank Sr. was a star who died young, so I guess not too many had the chance. Hank Williams and Jimmie Rodgers were the lynchpins of my father's interest in country music. In my father's world, an unwavering belief in and reverence for the power of music occupied the space society usually reserves for religion.

The rendition he did of the German love song "Lili Marlene" was emblematic of this belief. I'm not sure if he picked up the song while stationed in Germany or if he was even aware of the significance of the song. "Lili Marlene" was a song regularly broadcast during World War II from the Radio Belgrade radio station in Yugoslavia while it was under Nazi occupation. No one expected that a song could transcend conflict and war, yet the song—while undeniably German—was popular with British, American, and French as well as German soldiers. "Lili Marlene" was an unintentional anti-war anthem, embraced by nationalities engaged in war, which points to the power of music *über alles*.

4

Six-String Belief

STROBE LIGHTS

The teacher nodded her head slowly with feigned interest. "What kind of music does your band play?"

"Well, we play at parties so it's, uh . . . party music . . . sort of. This song's called 'Wild Thing' and this one's called 'All Day and All of the Night' and this one's called 'I Can't Explain' . . ."

The cassette demo tape of the band was not working any magic on the teacher as her mood turned from bemused interest to palpable disapproval. Our band's name was The Plebes, which referenced the underclass of Roman Society. The name was appropriate, but apparently our song selection and history of playing high school parties and dances was not resonating with the teacher in charge of booking the band for the eighth grade graduation party at Millstadt Consolidated School, where I was in seventh grade at the time.

I had started playing in the band in sixth grade, or around the age of eleven. The band was comprised of two of my older brothers (Wade and Dade) on lead vocals and bass guitar and myself, on electric guitar. The drummer position was filled by a succession of wild-spirited pugilists. It helped to have some muscle in the band, as alcohol, drugs, and fights would inevitably be part of the scene.

Not surprisingly, The Plebes did not play the graduation party that year, but perseverance and a politically savvy lineup change (adding an eighth grade drummer with insider connections at the school) got the band the coveted gig playing my own eighth grade graduation party. If those mundane institutional walls of that school could talk, they would tell of the exhilarating strobe-light garage-rock abandon that night. All in the same cafeteria where so many demoralized kids before and thereafter have trudged and will trudge up to the line with tray in hand to accept their daily portions scooped out from steaming vats of mediocrity . . .

THE M&O KID

James Crutchfield's prosthetic leg is on display at a bar in Benton Park. Not far away I saw James Crutchfield for the first time at an outdoor beer garden at Ninth and Allen. Just pay the cover and you're in. No fake ID necessary. It didn't matter—my Dad and brothers were there too. They all wanted to check out James Crutchfield—like a family affair of barrelhouse piano blues.

With the first strains echoing across this Soulard section of town it was abundantly clear that this guy was for real. James would hit the keys with repetitive outbursts of rhythm, resonance, and occasional flourishes of dissonance that was either an acknowledgement to jazz (Coltrane/Ornette Coleman) or was born out of the levee-camp barrelhouse gigs of his past.

What really mattered is that James had returned to performing. Through his music James brought clarity and an elevated spirit to those that came to see him play. No reciprocity in this world for James Crutchfield or countless other blues musicians who have died without a dollar or enough acclaim. James gave us the wisdom of his barrelhouse life in less-than-five-minute segments of pathos and raw power.

JAMES CRUTCHFIELD: RIP 1912-2001

*James played with:
Papa Lord God
Little Brother Montgomery
Champion Jack Dupree
Joe Pullum
Elmore James
Boyd Gilmore

1979

To this day I wonder what my parents were thinking as hour after hour of ear-splitting decibels of perfunctory rehearsals of punk and garage rock wailed and pounded out from their basement. There were no comments such as "Gang of Four ('I Found That Essence Rare') sounded real good today." But there was a quiet acceptance and approval of what was going down. How could there not be? My father had taught a few chords on guitar to some of the same neighborhood kids making the noisy music. As my father explained it, "I'd rather you guys be here making noise than someplace else making trouble."

ITALIAN GUITAR

When I think about a "first guitar," I realize there is some difficulty in qualifying which one was first. A handed-down guitar from my oldest brother John was chronologically my first. It was an early 1960s Gibson SG Special, which sounded great but had some tuning issues that earned it the nickname "Rubberneck." I had had enough handed-down clothes and longed for something to call my own. That longing for individuality—coupled with the tuning issues of Rubberneck—compelled me to start looking for a guitar to buy.

The band I was in at the time (The Primitives) was doing well. The band regularly rented an old German event hall (Das Liederkranz) in Millstadt, Illinois, where there was a cultural acceptance and willingness to look the other way when it came to underage folks drinking beer. This is a town after all that still devotes a festival once a year to beer (Bierfest). Thanks to the overwhelming German cultural influence of Millstadt and the help of the bass player's mother who collected money at the door, The Primitives were not only solvent but had some extra spending change. The proceeds from the first Liederkranz gig allowed for the search for a "first guitar" to begin in earnest.

I was about seventeen when I saw the newspaper ad for a used Vox V268 Ultrasonic guitar that had many unusual added features built in: an E tuner, a distortion booster, a hand activated wah-wah lever, and a tremolo switch. It was listed for $450 when it came out in 1968—about $2,900 in 2012 dollars. I paid $375 and got a lot of three-chord stomp mileage out of that first guitar, made by the good folks at the Vox factory in Recanati, Italy.

LEARNING THE GAME

I first became aware of the song "Learning the Game" by Buddy Holly not from his 1957 version, but rather from a bootleg recording of a sometimes rollicking yet also heartfelt Keith Richards banging out songs with a bottle of gin at Longview Farm Studio in Springfield, Massachusetts. Keith was apparently there to scope out the studio (complete with pond, stable, and horses) as a place for the Rolling Stones to rehearse for their 1981 U. S. Tour.

I was at Longview Farm a decade later recording Uncle Tupelo's "Still Feel Gone" when the engineers brought out the half-inch tape of Keith playing piano. On the tape Keith tackles Hoagy Carmichael's "Nearness of You," the Everly Brothers' "All I Have to Do Is Dream," Fats Domino's "Blue Monday," Jerry Lee Lewis's "Whole Lotta Shakin' Goin' On," "Apartment #9," which was made famous by Tammy Wynette (and supposedly written by Johnny Paycheck), and "Sing Me Back Home" by Merle Haggard. Keith was mixing his Teddy Boy roots with Bakersfield twang much the same way the ice cubes are mixing with gin in his audibly clinking glass as he exclaims on the tape, "I like this gin!"

To Keith it was just another day of checking out a space for the Stones to rehearse . . . but these songs documented on tape inspired me to "learn the game" . . .

P.S. Keith asserts in his book *Life* that the above recording was made in Toronto.

NEW ORLEANS

Disney World? Disney Land? It made no difference—as it wasn't part of my parents' plan. I would see neither as a kid. Instead, my folks took my brother and me to New Orleans during Mardi Gras.

We collected empty Jax and Dixie beer cans while the street winos slurped yesterday's grease out of large pots left on the sidewalk across from the St. Charles Hotel. The clatter and clang of the streetcar fused with "Gypsies, Tramps, and Thieves" forged the sonic backdrop as someone blasted the Cher song down the reverb streets. This was 1971, and I was five and my brother Wade was eight. New Orleans kept us alert from start to finish, but by far the most resonant memory we took back from the trip was of running out to the Mardi Gras parade and reaching our hands along the ground to pick up the beads that were thrown from the floats, only to promptly have our hands stomped on by the local street kids.

Isn't it a great metaphor for life—one that cannot be found at anything Disney? Life is a carnival that will unexpectedly stomp on you . . .

EIGHT-TRACK HEAVANA

I t was my second car and the year was 1983—and for a sixteen-year-old, a 1976 Pinto four-speed station wagon with a sun roof and an 8-track player was heaven and nirvana all rolled into one.

From somewhere I had acquired three 8-track tapes: The Ramones' *Road to Ruin*, Jimi Hendrix's *The Best of Jimi Hendrix*, and The Rolling Stones' *Sticky Fingers*. On the surface these three might seem mismatched or incongruous, but through repeated listenings, I found commonality and musical continuity with all three. The country-influenced "Questioningly" by The Ramones could sit next to The Rolling Stones' "Wild Horses," while the ethereal slide guitar of Ry Cooder on the Stones "Sister Morphine" was complimentary next to the incendiary Jimi Hendrix's "All Along the Watchtower."

It was all fortuitous for me that some Belleville person "upgraded" their muscle car sound system to cassette format and threw out their 8-track tapes. In actuality, 8-track tapes sounded much better. Whether the demise of the 8-track format was due to planned obsolescence and collusion amongst record companies to coerce people to buy cassettes or for simple reasons of convenience and size, I'm just glad I got to live my own slightly anachronistic 8-track era.

5

Catching an All-Night Station

A GIRLFRIEND

We were looking for some room to breathe. New Orleans had all the right elements: It was a culturally unique city that drew you in with music and charmed you with its cuisine before the final enticement of architecture and historical sense of place made you stay for good . . . or at least for a good while.

I was starting a new band called Son Volt which would not have been possible but for the fact that my girlfriend had a job and—most importantly—a credit card. The bulk of the recording expenses for the Son Volt recording "Trace" were put on that credit card. Preparing for the "Trace" recording meant driving the eleven hours from New Orleans to St. Louis to rehearse while other times driving a full twenty-four hours from New Orleans to Minneapolis for rehearsal.

All this time spent driving was actually fortuitous from a songwriting perspective as it gave plenty of time to reflect and create. The driving was not an impediment but rather the opposite in that it allowed creativity to flow without interruption.

In the mid 1990s, there was only so much music one could carry in the form of CDs and cassettes, so radio was a viable way to pass the time. There was an AM station that broadcast all night out of New Orleans (WLS "The Roadgang"), which propelled some of those drives and cemented the fiddle and steel guitar aesthetic in my mind as the right approach for "Trace."

The recording of "Trace" was done at what was essentially a home studio in Northfield, Minnesota—a city whose main claim to fame is that it fought back against the bank-robbing James Gang. As a person recording there, the most lasting impression was of the ubiquitous odor of the Malt-O-Meal factory, though the town itself was a studious yet bucolic place that treated and served our recording purposes well. The studio proprietor (Steve McKinstrey) had collected vintage microphones for years and had actually built the main recording console by hand.

To make this recording happen, I had driven a 1990 Honda Civic hatchback from New Orleans to St. Louis. In St. Louis, I packed the Honda Civic with a drum kit and amplifiers and attached a trailer behind full of more guitars and recording gear, and pulled it all up to Minneapolis and then back to St. Louis and New Orleans when the recording ended. Of course there must have been a better way than an economy car pulling a trailer. It was something the Honda guys could never have envisioned—that undersized car pulling a trailer the better part of the south-to-north distance of the United States to make a recording—but that's the way it happened.

BEVERLY LAUREL

"**H**ow safe is it to park the car here overnight?" asked the patron.

The desk clerk replied, "In twenty-five years, there have been only two items stolen out of parked cars: a laptop—and a sandwich . . ."

MIAMI, OKLAHOMA

Maybe it's because Jimmy used to be in a hair metal band. I prefer to think of it as a traditional "Easy Rider" culture-clash affair as opposed to some sort of post-9/11 hysteria. As the band's guitar tech, Jimmy had the all-black leather-and-dye look down so well he was often mistaken for a member of the Black Crowes.

We were hungry and needed gas, so we pulled off in Miami, Oklahoma, and gassed up, not realizing what we were about to set in motion. Next stop in town was a Taco Bell—an innocuous refuge, or so we thought. The small-town ladies working the counter immediately were engaged in conversation with Jimmy. This age-old dance was playing out as the rest of the band sat down to eat Taco Bell's proud offerings.

Concurrent with Jimmy's talking up the ladies on the inside was a strange "silent and dry" lightning storm happening outside. We all noticed it. "Weird storm out there . . ." The one person who apparently didn't notice the lightning outside was the Taco Bell manager, who had just walked in from outside. He immediately admonished the female employees for chatting with Jimmy as Jimmy sat down and joined the group. The rest of the meal went down without a hitch.

The next scene is me driving the band van out of the town of Miami, Oklahoma, when suddenly there is a police car behind us with lights flashing. The officer comes up to the driver side and asks for license and registration. He asks us what we are doing in Miami. We tell him we are a band that had just stopped for gas and food. Although we expected the worst, there was no drug sniffing dog or pat-downs.

Maybe the officer liked music, who knows?

As he let us go, he left us with this info to ponder: "We received a complaint call that a group of guys driving around in a van were taking pictures inside the Taco Bell." Of course no one in the band had a camera, and if they did, it would never have made it into a Taco Bell. Maybe the caller that made the complaint in Miami, Oklahoma, is now printing up bumper stickers that say: "Don't Talk to People and Keep Fear Alive . . ."

OXFORD

1992.

It was the kind of gig one could get used to. The Mississippi small-town, relaxed pace was omnipresent as you pulled in. With one panoramic gaze, the events to follow could be drawn into focus. First up and visible through the low branches and Spanish moss is the only late-night food option: fried chicken at the gas station. The venue is one block off the old square. Two blocks east of the square is the only hotel. Another block further is a cemetery with the unadorned and inconspicuous gravesite of William Faulkner.

The next morning (after the gig and the gas station) is the ascetic ritual of paying respects to the grave of Faulkner. Oxford and Faulkner had found symbiosis, as there would be no ostentatious gravestone, no tour buses, and usually not even a plastic flower. As the band pulls out of town toward the next gig, it's time to recap the events of the Oxford night.

"Who was that really drunk guy making noise?"

"Oh yeah, I remember he came up to the stage and wanted us to announce to everyone that he, Barry Hannah, had just arrived."

TAJ MAHAL

"**S**ince I laid my burden down . . ."

I got to know Taj Mahal in 1993 while on a multi-act traveling show. Taj was living in Tahiti at the time and was enthused about Hawaiian music. That was the greatest aspect about Taj—he was *always* enthused. If Taj was around he was either at the center of a backstage piano barrelhouse singalong or giving an impromptu tutorial about the slack-key tunings and pristine harmonics of the Hawaiian music he was listening to.

Our paths crossed again in 1997 when Son Volt and Taj Mahal shared a bill and a stage on the H.O.R.D.E. tour. On more than one occasion, the band would be on the bus and there would be a knock . . . "You fellas want Jerk? I've got salmon and I've got chicken . . ."

It was heaven-sent from the Hibachi grill of Taj Mahal, who expanded minds and palates like an unofficial ambassador. Nothing better in this world than touring with Taj . . .

MEMPHIS

I t was the first Mel Gibson movie I had ever made it through. Mel (as Robert the Bruce) gets beheaded at the end—the axe comes down, but mercifully the cinematographer does not show the mullet roll.

Robert the Bruce and freedom for the serfs all made sense to me as I used to know a Robert Bruce that lived at the top of a hill. He thought his job was to be king of his hill and to keep wayward serfs such as myself away. With this in mind . . . it was all about unwinding from ten hours of driving with a shot of Jim Beam in the hotel room when the night turned weird.

I heard the sound of cascading water coming from within the walls, so I checked the bathroom, and water was pulsating out of the roof over the shower and was running down the walls. It was late, so I grabbed some towels and made makeshift dykes and berms and went to sleep. That night I had a matter-of-fact dream about having drinks at a honky-tonk with Tom Waits.

I never caught up with clarity as I walked by a barker in a coffee-cup costume on that Memphis sidewalk morning . . .

BOBBY BLUE BLAND

The event was a blues festival in St. Louis, Missouri, in the early 1990s. It was an eclectic lineup that included the likes of Jerry Lee Lewis, St. Louis's own Henry Townsend, and Bobby Blue Bland.

Nothing prepared the uninitiated (my girlfriend and me) for the Bobby Blue Bland performance. Jerry Lee Lewis and Henry Townsend delivered what we expected, yet Bobby Blue Bland was another story . . .

In front of the stage, a veritable phalanx of large, age fifty-plus women enthusiastically responded to Bobby's music and stage presence. Ultimately, it was Bobby's vocal approximation of a pig snort that drove the ladies absolutely wild! Bobby Blue Bland still had that something . . .

6

Rhythm of the River

RIVERBEND

Leaving New Orleans was not an easy endeavor. The city was such a pulsating anomaly of extremes. It's the kind of place that will occupy your thoughts and will always pull you back.

On the day I was moving out of New Orleans, a profound lesson was learned—a musician's prerequisite (Musician's 101) kind of thing. I had picked up a hulking old Ludwig upright piano from a small town outside of New Orleans (Ponchatoula, Louisiana). There's a tipping point in the psyche of a twenty-something-year-old, and that is when rugged individualism and the casual intent to save money that would be spent on piano movers gets replaced by the more pervasive will to live and to not get crushed attempting to move heavy old pianos.

My fiancée and I were both positioned to absorb the "low side" of the piano's weight, while our ever-optimistic large-sized friend Keith manned the "high side" with a complex system of straps wrapped both around the piano and his full frame—all of which had us convinced that this would of course work perfectly. We only had to make it down three steps.

As the lesson unraveled, I learned that it only takes three steps to see your life and the lives of those you love flash before your eyes in an instant as the straps failed and team fiancée fell back under the unstoppable weight of a runaway upright piano. We were able to get out of the way as the momentum carried the piano a short distance before its legs buckled and brought it to a stop.

With bruises only to the piano, our pride, and our pocketbook ($150 to a piano moving company), that old piano from Ponchatoula and its particular brand of musicality lives on. It seems to be happiest when I play Professor Longhair's "Tipitina" or when my daughter plays "Dixie" . . .

1987

There was a trail of blood that led from the entry door and up the stairs and through the kitchen to the sofa where my father normally would be sleeping but which was now empty. Lying on the floor next to the sofa was a white denim Levi's jacket that was streaked with fresh blood stains.

This was the scene into which my mother awoke. This was 1987. I was twenty-one years old when I regained consciousness and climbed out of an upside-down 1978 Toyota Celica to find myself dazed and in pain (a broken nose and two broken ankles) but alive. I realized that I was in a field about a mile from my folks' home where I had started work as a fourteen-year-old baling hay and picking produce alongside Mexican migrants. I had fallen asleep at the wheel and hit the earthen embankment alongside the highway at fifty-five miles per hour, which launched me airborne and upside down into that afore-mentioned field of adolescent employment. Initially, I tried to flag down a passing car, but it was apparent that no one wanted to stop for a bloody stranger in the dark, so I was resigned to walking the mile home with both ankles broken.

Pop called the police and then took me to the accident scene, where I retrieved the cassette tape that I had been listening to when the accident happened. It had The Replacements on one side and Hüsker Dü on the other and bloodstains on both—so I kept the tape as a talisman for years. I was grateful (then and now) that no one else was hurt. Three months in a wheelchair ain't all bad. It gives one an opportunity to develop specialized skills like wheelchair wheelies. Like Woody Guthrie says, "Let your plans come out of mistakes."

HELL'S HAYRIDE

"Okay, everybody on . . . except the niggers." Thus began my first "hayride" with adults, alcohol, and recreational racism. Had the tractor driver fine-tuned that opening line—perhaps reworking it in his mind for maximum effect—or did he create it extemporaneously on the spot? It was immediately apparent that this hayride would not be like those of my youth, and a deep sense of foreboding settled in after that repugnant declaration to get on board. The concept of a hayride that was for adults and children was new to me, but this was Southern Illinois farm country, where tractors and trailers were plentiful and recreational racism was overtly alive and well.

The group I was with climbed aboard the second trailer that was to be pulled behind the tractor. Folks had brought coolers aboard, and at first my girlfriend and I sat on a cooler that was directly adjacent to the opening between the two trailers. It seemed a bit unstable with both of us there, so we moved to the hay bales near the center of the rear trailer. Tragically, the brother of my girlfriend took that spot on the cooler near the opening between the two trailers that we had vacated earlier. Suffice it to say, the hayride that had started with unsettling bigotry transitioned into gripping fear as the tractor reached speeds approaching thirty miles per hour, which caused the rear trailer to fishtail and jump, ultimately resulting in horror.

At first we felt the bumps—then the slow realization that the trailer had run over something. It was into pitch-black darkness that my girlfriend screamed, "Where's Mark?" We yelled at the driver repeatedly to stop. Finally, he stopped. We jumped off and ran about fifty yards back down the road to find Mark slumped in the street in extreme pain from internal bleeding. The second trailer had fishtailed and knocked Mark off-balance, which sent him under both sets of wheels of the trailer that the rest of us were riding on.

No one had cell phones in the early '90s so all the riders disembarked while the tractor driver sped off, pulling two empty trailers to get help from the nearest house. It seemed an interminable wait—maybe thirty minutes—before an ambulance reached the rural location.

When we arrived at the hospital, we were directed to an area outside an operating room where a doctor splattered in blood said it appeared that Mark was not going to make it, due to broken ribs and extensive internal bleeding, but that he was going to proceed with operating on Mark. The night was harrowing—but Mark eventually stabilized and survived.

Southern Illinois has left many scars, but we forgive. Life goes on.

TROUBLE IN THE HILLS

I overheard two novelists discussing the Ozarks and the overall perception of those who have never been there nor experienced it. They related a story of an NPR writer that rode a bike across the country but specifically avoided the Ozarks due to safety concerns. Hearing about this caused me to reflect on what I know firsthand about the Ozarks. I've traveled through the geographical area, but I've never lived there. What I do know about the Ozarks is from the post–World War II generation, who moved away from that region to find jobs at factories in places like Granite City, Illinois. Two Granite City guys transplanted from the Ozarks, my father and his old army buddy named Steve Krause, would reminisce about good times in the Army while stationed in Germany. They'd each brought back an accordion and an affinity for a few German songs. When these two got together, stories and songs were traded back and forth and the mood was generally festive. Sometimes the conversation turned to the Korean War and the mood got somber (especially for Steve, who saw combat and whose wartime injuries left him with a limp). The Korean War experience for my father was comparatively routine, as he was stationed on troop and supply transports at Inchon Harbor on the South Korean peninsula. I remember one of these get-togethers in particular between these two army buddies when the accordions did not come out of their cases and the talk was all serious. After Steve had left, I became curious. "What's wrong with Steve?" I asked. "They burned down his house," replied my father. "Who burned it down, and why?" I inquired. My father did his best to explain. "They burned down his house because he wasn't known to them, he wasn't part of their clan." So there it was, an explanation of a dark side of Ozark culture from my father, who understood its underlying individual idiosyncrasies and violence.

JOHN SMITH T

They say John Smith T was one bad fella. Fourteen men were said to have been killed in duels with Smith T, while other equally unfortunate souls were slain outright if John Smith T was in a bad temper or had been drinking, or both. He came to Missouri in 1797 with an insatiable appetite for land, lead mines, and guns. Smith T had a special nickname for his favorite rifle: "Hark from the Tombs." The main adversary of John Smith T was Moses Austin (father of Stephen Austin of Texas), and their battle for dominance of the lead mining district evolved to include militias equipped with customized guns and, in the case of Moses Austin, a prominently displayed cannon. I came across the legend of John Smith T while researching my own ancestral history in the lead mining district of southeast Missouri.* Around 1830, these Farrar ancestors were neighbors of John Smith T. As far as I can tell, none of my ancestors were killed by Smith T, but who knows? There's no way of knowing if they ever saw the wrong side of "Hark from the Tombs" . . .

* I found this information in *Dick Steward's Frontier Swashbuckler: The Life and Legend of John Smith T*, published by the University of Missouri in 1999.

THE WRONG KIND OF WHEELS

For several years musician friends from Vermont were singing the praises of driving a used Volvo station wagon. A Volvo had "safest car on the road" status with enough room to haul guitars, amplifiers, and whatever else. Who could argue with mechanized leather seats, power windows, and seat warmers, even if all that stuff was about seven to ten years old by the time a musician could afford a used Volvo?

In Vermont, Volvos are so ubiquitous they are "like the state bird," to quote a musician friend. So I capitulated and bought a 1988 740 station wagon. This decision would play out in ways I had never imagined. It's true that I was aware that I was living in the home state of Rush Limbaugh (there is now a statue of him at the state capitol). Also true that Missouri was the scene of the most violent guerilla warfare during the Civil War, the aftereffects of which are manifest in a sort of chronic-urban-versus rural identity struggle that is still playing out.

I began to realize all of this one day while driving on Interstate 55 when a guy in an old pickup truck pulled alongside and screamed something at me, though what he was saying was lost in interstate noise. Before I could discern what he was saying, he began to make swerving motions with his car directed at the Volvo and finished up by throwing his water bottle, which glanced off the Volvo's front windshield.

Okay, just an isolated incident, I thought. Nope. Next time it's on Interstate 270. No yelling this time as this (different) guy goes straight to trying to run the Volvo off the road. What the fuck? There were no "Coexist" bumper stickers on this Volvo (yet).

After countless other incidents of middle fingers raised at the Volvo wagon, I began to realize that my Vermont Yankee friends had steered me wrong. I did keep that car for years and actually bought another Volvo wagon and drove that too until I needed more space for hauling musicians and equipment, so I bought a two-ton truck. In Missouri, it seems, the "safest car on the road" is a truck . . .

STRANGE OLD ST. LOUIS

St. Paul Sandwich (egg foo young between two slices of white bread with mayonnaise, pickle, and tomato)

Slinger (two eggs, one hamburger patty, hash browns, cheese, and onions, with chili slung over all)

Toasted Ravioli (deep-fried meat-filled pasta)

Mostaccioli (large tubular pasta, meat, and red sauce)

Provel Cheese (local processed-cheese version of provolone)

Brain Sandwich (sautéed cow brains)

7

Americana Technicolor

DIALECTIC OF COUNTRY AND COMMUNISM

• COUNTRY MUSIC •	• COMMUNISM •
1917 Folklorist Cecil Sharp publishes the comprehensive study *English Folk Songs from the Southern Appalachians*	**1917** October Revolution in Russia sees the establishment of the world's first communist state
1922 Victor and Okeh labels record the first country artists	**1922** Joseph Stalin is named General Secretary of the Communist Party in the Soviet Union
1923 Hank Williams Sr. is born	**1923** Vladimir Lenin suffers a debilitating stroke
1924 Vernon Dalhart records "Wreck of the Old '97" and radio station WLS begins broadcast of *National Barn Dance*	**1924** Lenin dies
1925 *Grand Ole Opry* is first broadcast on November 28, 1925	**1926** Fidel Castro is born
1927 Ralph Peer records *The Carter Family and Jimmie Rodgers*	**1927** Chinese Communist Party (CCP) is outlawed in China
	1931 Mikhail Gorbachev is born
1939 *Grand Ole Opry* begins its first network broadcast on NBC	**1939** Coalition including communists surrenders in Spain
1943 Al Dexter records "Honky Tonk Blues"	**1943** Communism is established in Poland
1946 Ernest Tubb has hit song "Drivin' Nails in My Coffin" while Al Dexter has hit with "Wine Women and Song"	**1946** Stalin makes speech saying, "Capitalism and communism are incompatible." Also Winston Churchill makes Iron Curtain Speech

(cont'd. on next page)

(cont'd. from previous page)

• COUNTRY MUSIC •	• COMMUNISM •
1947 Hank Williams signs with MGM	**1947** "Hollywood Ten" are blacklisted by the U. S. House Committee on Un-American Activiteis
1948 The Louisiana Hayride begins in Shreveport, Louisiana	**1948** Communists take Czechoslovakia
1949 Hank Williams plays the *Grand Ole Opry*; encores "Lovesick Blues" multiple times	**1949** Mao Zedong takes control and establishes "People's Republic of China"
1950 "I'm Movin' On" is a number-one hit for Hank Snow	**1950** Communist forces of North Korea invade South Korea
1953 Hank Williams dies on New Year's Day	**1953** Stalin dies
1954 "Slowly" by Webb Pierce incorporates and ushers in a new style of pedal steel as played by Bud Isaacs	**1954** Dien Bien Phu: French surrender to communist forces in Vietnam
1957 George Jones has a hit with "Don't Stop the Music" and Ray Price has a hit with "You Done Me Wrong"	**1957** Russian satellite "Sputnik" is successfully launched
1959 Lefty Frizzell has a hit with "Cigarettes and Coffee Blues"	**1959** Cuba is taken over by Fidel Castro
	1960 USAF U-2 spy plane is shot down in Soviet Union airspace. Pilot Francis Gary Powers survives
1961 Billy Ray Cyrus is born	**1961** Bay of Pigs operation fails
1962 Garth Brooks is born	**1962** Cuban missile crisis occurs
1963 Patsy Cline, Hawkshaw Hawkins, and Cowboy Copas die	**1963** Lee Harvey Oswald poses for photo holding two Marxist newspapers, *The Militant* and *The Worker*
1964 Buck Owens has a number-one hit with "Together Again"	**1964** Gulf of Tonkin incident sets stage for Vietnam War

• COUNTRY MUSIC •

1968 Merle Haggard has number-one hit with "Sing Me Back Home"

1972 Buck Owens has a number-one hit with "Made In Japan"

1976 Waylon Jennings and Willie Nelson have a number-one hit with "Good Hearted Woman"

1980 George Jones has a number-one hit with "He Stopped Loving Her Today"

1981 Merle Haggard has a number-one hit with "I Think I'll Just Stay Here and Drink"

1985 George Strait has a number-one hit with "Does Fort Worth Ever Cross Your Mind"

1989 Garth Brooks releases his eponymous album

1991 Garth Brooks releases "Ropin' The Wind"

• COMMUNISM •

1968 Soviet Red Army moves into Czechoslovakia

1972 Nixon visits China

1976 Chinese Communist leader Mao Zedong dies

1980 Lech Walesa negotiates Gdansk Agreement in Poland

1981 Martial law is declared in Poland

1985 Mikhail Gorbachev initiates "Glasnost" and "Perestroika"

1989 The Berlin Wall falls

1990 Communist East Germany and Capitalist West Germany reunite

1991 The Communist Soviet Union is dissolved

CAPTAIN JACK

Captain Jack is the only person I've ever met who bought an entire town.

I had arranged to look at an old grand piano that was advertised for sale in the paper when I was greeted at the door of the agreed-upon address by a disheveled older fellow with an outstretched hand, who curiously introduced himself as "Captain Jack."

As I was giving the piano a test run, Captain Jack noticed my interest in the multitude of model jet planes in various stages of completion that were strewn about his house. "I was a pilot, and I was awakened one morning and given a secret mission that ultimately involved me flying a fighter jet though a hydrogen bomb mushroom cloud," Captain Jack explained. "They wanted to see if it could be done and if there were any adverse effects."

As I continued to test out the piano, he interrupted and handed me a newspaper article about the town he owned in rural Missouri, near New Florence. The "town" consisted of a gas station, an abandoned school, and a church. A photo of a church atop a flat-bed semi accompanied the article, which went on to explain that Captain Jack had the church lifted and moved on a truck to the same side of the street as his gas station and school building.

This was Captain Jack's world, and I became a part of it when I purchased the piano. I've never had it tested for radiation, but I did record one song on it: "Sultana."

MELUNGEONS

T hey say Abe Lincoln and Elvis Presley were both Melungeons . . .

Melungeons? The first time I heard the word was in 1997, while in Knoxville, Tennessee, for a performance. I overheard the promoter talking about a book he was reading called *Melungeons Yesterday and Today* by Jean Bible, which told of a mysterious people who appeared in Appalachia in the 1700s. The promoter gave me the book, which I promptly read while on the road, though I subsequently moved on to other books and endeavors.

While researching family history fourteen years later, I came across the term *Melungeon* again, which led to the book *The Melungeons: The Resurrection of a Proud People*, by Brent Kennedy. In his book, Kennedy purports that Melungeon ancestry includes Portuguese, Spaniards, Turks, Moors, Jews, Native Americans, Africans, and various Europeans. No one knows the exact derivation of the term *Melungeon*, but several theories persist. One theory is that the word is derived from the French word *mélange*, meaning "mixture." Another is that *Melungeon* comes from the Turkish words *melun can*, which translates to "lost souls," with that theory asserting that Melungeons could be descendants of shipwrecked Turkish or Moorish sailors. Sir Francis Drake reportedly furloughed and released Turks and Moors from a captured Spanish ship to the coast of North Carolina. Who knows? None of these theories and assertions can be proven.

What can be proven is that the late, formative years of the United States were fraught with unconscionable discrimination and cruel anti-miscegenation laws. Walter Ashby Plecker was the head of the state of Virginia's Bureau of Vital Statistics from 1912 to 1946. Plecker believed "there is a danger of the ultimate disappearance of the white race in Virginia and the country." The state of Virginia agreed and passed the "Racial Integrity Act of 1924," which categorized all "non-whites" as "colored" and further criminalized marriages between "whites" and "non-whites." Being designated "colored" meant one was subject to Jim Crow laws.

Ultimately the question becomes whether the term Melungeon has any relevance. Yes, to those who were discriminated against in the hills of Appalachia. Any relevance to me? No, I'm just another mongrel in what Bob Dylan and Little Walter call "this crazy mixed up world."

TALE OF TWO RODENTS

I've always struggled to reconcile the idea that we have poison and guillotine traps for some rodents while at the same time we buy elaborate cages and food to treat others like rodent royalty. Pet store for food . . . hardware store for poison.

Two of the lucky pet-store variety won the lottery. A nice double cage to house them and name-brand food to feed them. These two gerbils, however, exhibited radically different ethos. The brown and white gerbil (Two-Tone) was industrious (always working out on the wheel) and seemed more than content to have food and a roof over his head. Not so with his brother (Snowy). He seemed to be either silently contemplating an escape plot or actively probing the perimeter of the cage for escape ideas.

Eventually the scheming and diligence paid off for Snowy. The cage lid was left unlatched, and he made his break. His brother Two-Tone, however, was found the next morning with his head poking out of the cage as if frozen by fear and indecision.

Snowy was spotted later that evening in the living room. All hands on deck! Two parents, two children (seven and ten), equipped with butterfly nets and badminton rackets. Snowy had chosen to make his final freedom stand underneath a sofa. Every time we made a move, Snowy made an effective counter-move. Only a coordinated operation ("right flank—center—left flank . . . NOW!") proved successful against the elusive and ever-resourceful Snowy.

Unfortunately Snowy did not live much longer in captivity (though he did feel the freedom of Papillon for one day). Meanwhile, his hard-working brother Two-Tone is like a gerbil Jack LaLanne— defying the average life expectancy for his kind.

STAN KANN THE GADGET MAN

I never knew Stan, but I used to live down the street from where he lived, and we'd give each other a nod and a hello as we passed each other while out walking about.

Stan seemed both diminutive and confident, so it's no surprise that he could alternately crawl inside an old Wurlitzer theater organ to fix it or make people laugh on talk shows. They say Stan appeared on *The Tonight Show* with Johnny Carson seventy-seven times while explaining his various esoteric devices.

For twenty-two years, Stan was the Wurlitzer organ player at the Fox Theater in St. Louis, back when organ music preceded the featured movie and filled the intermission. Most of all, Stan was known for having the largest collection of vintage vacuum cleaners in the world. That statistic in and of itself demands respect.

THE PORTER

What are the odds? The Porter was tall, about six foot six, while I measure out at about six feet standing. Maybe that six-inch differential accounts for something. I was standing about three feet away. Perhaps someone really well versed in math could devise an equation that could explain it all based on the height difference and distance between the Porter and myself.

Everyone will find themselves in a truly absurd moment of disbelief at least once . . . I did. It went down on a cross-country Amtrak train trip with my family. We were boarding in Galesburg, Illinois, and the occasion was all smiles and excitement of a journey about to begin when the unexpected event occurred midway through the Porter's laconic introduction.

As the Porter's arm swung around with pointer finger extended, it all happened in an instant. The cold, salty-metallic-microbial horror . . . The Porter had just stuck his finger in my mouth as he was pointing us in the direction of our cabin. The Porter continued on with his spiel without missing a beat.

At first I tried to envision what Larry David would do. Revenge? Nah . . . I'll just offer up advice: If you find yourself on a train with a tall porter, just bob and weave like Cassius Clay . . .

BUDDY RICH

The first concert I went to as a kid of about eight years of age was Buddy Rich. How could I have known that the aging man with the awesome haircut and paradiddles would prove so valuable later in my life as an antidote to boredom?

Since being in a band involves ten percent playing music and ninety percent waiting around to play music, there is a need for comic relief, and Buddy Rich unwittingly provided that service.

Buddy was known for hiring young band members and berating and threatening them while offstage. (Buddy was a black belt in karate.) As a result, the beleaguered band members began surreptitiously recording Buddy's rants.

"I'm out there trying to do somebody a fucking favor and you motherfuckers are sucking all OVER the place . . ." "Get off my fucking bus . . ." "I'm gonna replace you motherfuckers with an all-L.A. band tonight—try me . . . ASSHOLES . . ."

P.S. I had a cab driver in L.A. once who claimed to have been Buddy Rich's driver for years. "Yeah, Buddy . . . all he would ever eat was Chinese food—nothing else . . ."

OPERATION KITCHEN FLOOR

When the hermit crab gets loose and the word on the street is that an escapee hermit crab will be a dead hermit crab within days that will permeate all living quarters with a putrid overpowering stench of death, then, naturally, this is a search-and-rescue operation for Dad.

There is one weakness of the escapee crab that can be exploited, and that is the distinctive *clik-tckk* of the hermit crab shell hitting the floor and just about everything else as it ambles around. The crab's climb to freedom gives it many inherent advantages though, such as—what room?

With a sleeping bag and a flashlight, I chose the kitchen as a base for the hermit crab stakeout. The hermit crab that was named (Thunderstrike) by my son Ethan was captured that night in the kitchen. Thunderstrike lived to see retirement and passed on with a full-honors burial.

THE PROCESS

I always looked to Gertrude Stein, Jack Kerouac, William Burroughs, and Charles Bukowski for inspiration. If you are going to work creatively within a medium, you have to bend the rules of the medium to be challenged and inspired.

Gertrude was there first and probably caught the most flak as a result. By rearranging the established order of words, Gertrude was able to breathe new life and meaning into language by challenging readers to assign their own individualistic meanings to her impressionistic words.

Jack Kerouac took matters a step further by blending linear prose with a stream-of-consciousness approach that embraced the rhythms and improvisation of jazz. William Burroughs brought out the "cut up" method, which showed that the random juxtaposition of words was the ultimate test of finding new, unexpected meaning in language.

Charles Bukowski gives maybe the best paradigm of all through perseverance. Just create whatever the hell you want, and in the process you will find your own voice, and you'll either die or people will take notice.

MCSORLEY'S

Known as "the oldest Irish bar in New York City," McSorley's stands as a resilient reminder of old New York. Two kinds of beer are for sale—"light" and "dark," with the "light" being a bit on the dark side and the "dark" a darker shade than the light but a similar-tasting beer. It's also curious to note that at McSorley's, ordering "a beer" means two draft mugs slapped down on a bar counter made smooth from centuries of brew and humanity.

There's a story behind every artifact and ornament adorning the walls—most of which pre-date the 1940s. There's a photograph of Woody Guthrie holding court with his signature "this machine kills fascists" guitar in hand. When asked, the bartender will dutifully show off the Woody Guthrie photo in the back room just above the fireplace. Without missing a beat, said bartender will then take you a couple steps away from the Woody Guthrie photo and will proudly show you a photo of Larry Hagman.

All of this leaves one to ponder how celebrity alone equates the two and what would Woody Guthrie think if he knew?

8

The Road is a Spiderweb on the Map

TEXAS LAMENT

Townes gave us riches and Townes gave us treasure in the form of life's experience put to song.

It hit me like a proverbial ton on bricks when I first heard the music of Townes Van Zandt. Townes was a perfect find—he was like an amalgam of the aesthetic of Bob Dylan and Ramblin' Jack Elliott with some Texas mysticism thrown in for good measure. It was at the Maple Leaf Bar on Oak Street in New Orleans in 1995 where I first saw Townes—who incidentally was sharing the bill with Ramblin' Jack Elliott.

Both Townes and Jack had flown in to do the gig (Townes from Europe), so they both had the aura of traveling troubadours as they set up side by side, cross-legged on the floor with their guitars, guitar cases, harps, harp holders, and capos—*de rigueur* folk stuff. They alternated singing songs, with the one not singing sitting quietly in a meditative repose, and occasionally they joined together for a spontaneous sing-along.

Several years later on a Son Volt tour, the band had a day off in Philadelphia, which coincided with two shows that Townes was scheduled to do in Bethlehem, Pennsylvania. We arrived in time to catch a few songs at the end of Townes's first show, which were deftly executed—especially the Lightnin' Hopkins–inspired finger-picking style. Anticipation for more transcendent music for the second show beat a slow retreat as Townes took the stage and announced that he had indulged in some whiskey at the bar across the street between shows.

Finding the right balance of respect for the man and his body of work juxtaposed with his current condition and cavalier disregard for putting on a show was difficult to reconcile. Townes's road manager put us on the list and arranged for us to meet Townes after the show. I was struggling with the traditional roles of mentor and student being turned on their heads. I felt like saying to Townes, "The whiskey made you mess up your songs, and your songs are paramount." Of course I didn't say it, and it wouldn't have mattered. Whether by choice or by constructs of DNA, Townes's path was already well charted.

I never knew if Townes was aware of my music, but he greeted me warmly with a smile and an outstretched hand. Our meeting was brief—as I am always at a loss for words when around people whose work I admire. At one point Townes said, "Are you taking care of yourself?" I didn't respond with what I was thinking, which was, "Are *you* taking care of *yourself*?" The irony and impact of his question has never left me. Part of me wanted to stay and soak up the paradoxical magic of Townes, but the part of me that wanted to keep the image of the master songwriter of the heart intact (the way he is on recordings) won out.

As our van pulled out of Bethlehem, I glimpsed a brief image through an open door to a bar where Townes had gone—belly up, glass raised—living life his way . . .

THE BAND

In 1993 Uncle Tupelo played a week's worth of shows as part of a multi-act traveling road show that included The Band, Taj Mahal, and Michelle Shocked. As a twenty-five-year-old, I reveled in the moment and experience of being around musicians that had paid their dues and who possessed an effortless musical ability as a result.

Garth Hudson: "It's an indigent general"—speaking matter-of-factly about his rented keyboard for the evening's show. Garth kept to himself for most of the tour, and in retrospect, that idea had its merits. Garth was both approachable and quick to strike up a conversation when he was around.

Levon Helm: "You boys want some of this smoke? Just elbow your way on in there, son . . ." Everyone knows of the musical powers of Levon Helm. Levon's character and soul were the driving force and backbone of The Band. They were once called Levon and the Hawks for this indisputable reason.

Rick Danko: Getting to hear the crystalline voice of Rick Danko sing "It Makes No Difference" during soundcheck for a week in a variety of cavernous theaters and clubs was a transcendent experience. Rick was fresh out of rehab for the beginning of the tour. Upon seeing our guitar tech drinking a Crazy Horse forty-ounce beer, Rick approached and exclaimed, "Man, I just got out of rehab—I gotta have some of that."

He then proceeded to take a long swig of Crazy Horse—probably for effect—and to strike up a sense of camaraderie with the upstarts in the opening band. I never saw Rick indulge in anything else for the duration of the tour except the haunting music he was known for.

Touring with The Band was an invaluable apprenticeship—a fundamental stage that provided a foundational inspiration for these touring wheels to turn . . .

JUNE CARTER

"Hey John—I want you to meet these nice boys," said June Carter with a smile. "They play one of A. P.'s songs ("No Depression in Heaven")."

Rewind to high school in the early 1980s, when I had the VCR set to record vintage *Grand Ole Opry* shows from the 1950s that broadcast every morning at 5:00 AM. The shows were filmed in vivid, saturated color, and most of the country stars of the day paraded through, from George Jones to Ernest Tubb to the Carter Family to bluegrass's Bill Monroe. In a black-and-white clip from early 1952 (*Kate Smith Evening Hour*), June Carter introduces Hank Williams Sr. and clowns around with him before he launches into "Hey Good Lookin'."

Fast forward to 1993. "John, it was so nice to hear these boys play tonight. Hey, we're having a (Johnny Cash sixty-first) birthday party this weekend in Nashville, and we'd like you boys to come." We were moved by the openhearted invitation yet crushed by the realization that we were on the West Coast with over a week's worth of shows to do.

If only there could be more June Carters in the world . . .

KEITH RICHARDS

I met Keith Richards at a photo shoot for a Gram Parsons tribute concert in L. A. in 2004. Later in the evening, my wife Monica and daughter Ava joined the backstage rehearsal show melee. Ava no doubt was unsure of all the Nudie suits and noise, so she started to cry—at which point Keith strolled over to comfort her and said, "Ah—looks like somebody missed their sleepy time." Keith's finest moment . . .

It was all a good time on a grand scale celebrating Gram's musical legacy with Jim James, John Doe, Norah Jones, Lucinda Williams . . . the list goes on. At the end, I fell into a Zelig moment by making a pre-arranged deal to switch with the house band piano player midway through the finale of "Wild Horses" and play the last half. For half a song, I felt I knew what it was like to be Woody Allen *and* Jim Dickinson . . .

BILL MONROE

No one disputes that all bluegrass roads lead back to one man: Bill Monroe. This venerable progenitor of a uniquely vibrant encapsulation of American culture and sound did a free weekly gig at a small club outside of Nashville for the love of the music he is credited with creating—as well as complimentary steak.

I was there with a drummer friend from Nashville as Bill took the stage. His towering presence and command of the mandolin—that instrument that *really* drives the musical genre we know as bluegrass—was a true spiritual offering. Bill was up in years, and to witness his dexterity and commitment at his age was inspiring.

Then it was dinnertime, and Bill left the stage with hand outstretched to greet the flock before he sat down to eat his steak. Any man that used to challenge local toughs to bare-knuckle fistfights before a gig as a way to alleviate the monotony of touring must be revered . . .

SAN ANTONE

"**O**kay, let's get this one, boys!" With these words, Doug Sahm solidified the desire of one young musician to chase the transformative healing power of music.

Doug's life was a cross-stitch of fact and legend. They say Doug played a demonstrative lap steel for Hank Williams at the age of eleven. His band, the Sir Douglas Quintet, rode the wave of Beatlemania by only having a silhouette photo on their album so as not to give away the fact that they were a band comprised of multi-ethnic TexAmericanos and not British, as their early sound would suggest.

Doug's conviction and enthusiasm for music was palpable, contagious, and always audible. In 1994, while recording with Uncle Tupelo, Doug hit a microphone stand with his guitar headstock (which can be heard on the recording) while getting into the groove. But no matter— it's all about the groove anyway. That was the lesson learned.

After recording "Key to My Heart" with Doug, our paths would cross many times over the years when passing through Austin with Son Volt. Doug would often stop by the gig to give words of encouragement as well as to join the band onstage for "Key to My Heart" or "She's About a Mover." The effect of Doug onstage with Son Volt in Austin always created a level of intensity that can only happen with the right chemistry of band, mentor, and audience, but it was ultimately the charisma of Doug that made those sit-ins special for all involved.

Doug and I exchanged phone numbers a couple of times, and, on occasion, Doug left long messages on my voicemail machine. It was unmistakable and somewhat surreal: that Texas hepcat drawl on my answering machine, singing praises for the song "Tear Stained Eye" and suggesting we co-write songs. It was profoundly inspirational as a student of Doug's work.

We never did co-write; I sent him a verse and a chorus of "Hanging Blue Side," but nothing ever came of it. I later donated the answering machine that Doug left his messages on to charity. Maybe now there is a kid in a Third World country thinking, *Who is this Doug?*

FALLING CARS

The cars from my youth were either from a junkyard or soon headed there. Hanging around salvage yards became a commonplace childhood experience. My father would take me along to Mudd Duck Salvage and Granite City Salvage yards—though when I was young, I had to wait in the car while he poked around the junk heaps. "Too dangerous," claimed my father. "Falling cars and junkyard dogs." Fair enough. By high-school age I was driving cars that were rescued from salvage, much the same way pets are saved by animal shelters. I was thankful for these refurbished junkers, as a car meant freedom, and with these junkers, I had that.

The junkyard-ethos era with my father continued on through my early twenties, till I had enough money to buy a car outside of the salvage realm. I was in a touring band then, in the early 1990s. The last junkyard sojourn with my father was on the same day I left that touring band for the second time. The first time was when the bass player woke up my girlfriend, who was sleeping on the back equipment van bench, to profess his love for her while I was in charge of driving up front. The reason for leaving the band the aforementioned second time was for artistic and band direction differences of opinion. I spoke the words, "I have the desire to be your friend. It's just not possible in the context of this band." The bass player responded with belligerent vitriol. I walked away . . . Even then I was aware that nothing in the world could be more pathetic than two guys throwing punches in the early afternoon in a decrepit apartment on Eleventh Street in Belleville, Illinois.

The band owed management a lot of money, which necessitated an extension of a touring-and-paying-off-debt period, which ultimately led to the dissolution of the group. The band's manager had the members over to his house after the band's final gig. "You guys should shake hands and say goodbye," volunteered the manager. The bass player and I then shook hands. I said, "Good luck," as the bass player said nothing in response.

After this exchange, the mood was awkward as I said goodbye to the other contemporaneous members of the band, while the bass player monitored closely with a proprietary presence. (Other erroneous accounts have emphasized this uneasy moment while leaving out the handshake and "good luck" part.)

Many years later, I revisited the Granite City Salvage yard. The experience was imbued with an overall sense of decaying nostalgia. So it goes for worn out cars and old bands.

ROGER MCGUINN

t was 1996, and Roger McGuinn had me over for dinner.
In retrospect I see that it was an extremely selfless, be-
nevolent gesture on his part. Roger and I were to "inter-
view" each other for a magazine article, and he could have chosen
a Waffle House or a Denny's or refused the whole idea, but fortunately he didn't. If he had, I would have missed seeing his tricked-out
touring van with a GPS satellite receiver on top (nobody had GPS in
1996!) and his vintage Rickenbacker 360 twelve-string that was used
to record the intro riff to "Mr. Tambourine Man."

I was not yet born when The Byrds' "Mr. Tambourine Man" was
recorded, but that intro was one of the first riffs that I learned on
guitar more than a decade later. Roger left me with this advice which
to date I have not yet heeded: "I like what you're doing and keep with
it . . . but don't bother with the country stuff." Even though I haven't
been following his face-to-face advice, I have been following Roger's
recorded music since I was old enough to turn on an AM transistor
radio. This one's for you, Roger . . .

PALACE HOTEL

Some might say *gaudy* and some might say *Gaudi*, but the old Palace Hotel in North Bergen, New Jersey, had character. The opulent but tired decor at least transported one from the monotony of corporate homogeneity found in the hotels of America. The Palace was the kind of place you could meet Smokin' Joe Frazier dressed to the nines (we did) and rehearse and write songs without bothering anybody. It was a respite from the frenetic pace of Manhattan as well as a chance to appreciate a slice of Jersey. The original Palace Hotel is no more, so it's up to those with memories to recount because those renovated walls won't talk . . .

9

The Salt and the Steel of the Breath

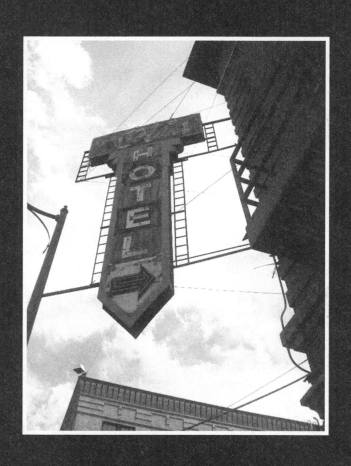

JELLY JAW

I think about Henry Townsend. Henry was on his own by the age of ten, when he hopped an Illinois freight train from Cairo to East St. Louis to find out what the world had to offer.

For Henry, singing became a means to survive. An old St. Louis neighborhood known as "Bucket of Blood" is where Henry later played house parties and sold moonshine. On the streets of St. Louis, Henry took an ice pick to the hand from a jealous lover, and from an adversarial blues singer named Jelly Jaw, Henry took a knife in the back. In retaliation, Henry borrowed a pistol and shot Jelly Jaw, relieving his adversary of one of his testicles.

Through it all, Henry persevered and along the way gave us his version of life, his visceral, open-tuned manifesto distilled into two minutes of vision and truth: "Jack O' Diamonds Georgia Rub," 1931.

BENNIE'S BLUES

The hat perched atop his head was a Greek sailor's cap. The instrument in his hands was an inexpensive, imported, knock-off guitar. The amplifier he played through was a solid-state model most guitar players considered anathema to a good sound. But Bennie Smith proved that it was all about the player and not the equipment. With cool aplomb he delivered quintessential electric blues that could transcend notions of time and space. At the Wednesday night jam session at a cafe across the interstate came the pungent breeze of hops in progress from the world's leading brewery, providing an olfactory support to these blues. Wherever one wanted to go or to get away from . . . Bennie Smith could take you there for three hours on a Wednesday night . . .

ALEX CHILTON

"**A**lex Chilton is coming by to borrow my feather duster . . ."

It's 1996, and Son Volt is recording at Chez Flames Studio (owned and operated by Keith Keller) in New Orleans. While cutting a version of "Looking at the World Through a Windshield," the phone rings. It's Alex, and he wants to come by and borrow a feather duster.

Alex and Keith Keller were New Orleans compadres, and this sort of episode was not unusual. We in the band were all too content to take a break and meet perhaps the most enigmatic yet talented songwriter and recording artist this side of the Beatles. We all said hello, and the feather duster handoff went down without a hitch.

Ten years later, Alex and I paid our respects to our mutual friend Keith Keller at a full-honors jazz funeral procession (led by the Treme Brass Band) in the French Quarter of New Orleans. The last time I saw Alex was in 2008 when we shared a bill at a festival in St. Louis. We briefly reminisced about Keith and exchanged phone numbers.

Two years later, on March 17, I was on the California Zephyr outside of Reno, Nevada, retracing the tracks that Jack Kerouac took from Chicago to San Francisco in his novel *Big Sur*, when I got a call from a friend in London saying Alex had died. Just hours before—on the train on the flats by the Great Salt Lake of Utah—I had been listening, mesmerized, and repeating Alex's masterpiece songs over and over—songs that had recently been released on the box set (*Keep an Eye on the Sky*) and sounded cogent, relevant, and new.

Alex Chilton RIP.

SESTO CALENDE

There was something intriguing about Carlo Carlini . . . For starters, he claimed that he used to work with Colonel Gaddafi in Libya back in the 1960s and 1970s when Libya still had ties to its former colonizer, Italy. Carlo got drafted for service in the Italian Army and was stationed in Libya to build roads for the Colonel (a.k.a. the Chairman of the Revolutionary Command Council of Libya).

By the 1980s, Carlo had become a promoter of American singers and songwriters. Just about anyone from Townes Van Zandt to Alejandro Escovedo had done tours with Carlo. Sesto Calende (in Northern Italy) was where Carlo lived and based his operations, where his dealings with musicians allowed him to wear the various hats of music promoter, driver, magician, raconteur, and self-appointed agent to celebrate Italian culture.

A staccato burst of "*Caffè?*" from Carlo meant that a double shot of espresso must be consumed pronto by all parties or Carlo would be disappointed. Breakfast consisted of wine, pasta, and more espresso.

"Italians invented food," proclaimed Carlo with a self-assured smile.

We Americanos agreed, even while harboring the thought that we'd sprint for an Americana safe-house à la McDonalds if we saw one. At a music festival in an old quarry off the banks of Lake Maggiore, I saw Carlo Carlini for the last time . . . He was smiling, of course. His enthusiasm and support of American music will be sorely missed . . .

RALPH MOONEY

It could be argued that Ralph Mooney is one of the most underrated, under-appreciated, and gifted musicians of all time. The transcendent pedal steel guitar accompaniment that Ralph contributed to recordings by Buck Owens, Wynn Stewart, and Waylon Jennings is unequaled in its inventiveness and scale of output. Ralph was originally an electric lead guitar player, and his approach to playing pedal steel embodied this explosive style and analogous driving spirit. Ralph was a co-writer of the song "Crazy Arms," which was a hit for both Ray Price and Patsy Cline. Through the power of his pen and his pedal steel guitar, Ralph Mooney owned the scene as the primary progenitor of Honky Tonk . . .

10

The Speculation Din

FREAK SHOW

Musicians are basically cut from the same cloth as carnies. Whoever puts on the biggest freak show wins the prize. Folk songs were taught to me on harmonica by my father at the age of four. I learned about public performance and the feelings of ambivalence that go with it at the age of five.

The kindergarten class I was in was scheduled to sing a song for a school assembly (grades K through eight) for parents and students. The teacher asked if anyone played an instrument. I volunteered that I played the harmonica, so it was arranged that I would give a solo performance as the last act at the assembly. The chosen song was "Oh Susannah," and after the last note, the place erupted with electrified applause. Suddenly there were teachers, parents, and older kids in my face, patting me on the back vociferously.

Equal parts elation and horror: That's how one gets started in the circus . . .

CHUCK BERRY

It was kind of surreal to see Chuck Berry in the audience at a Hüsker Dü show at the club Mississippi Nights in the 1980s. The guy I was with was being effusive and enthusiastically asked Chuck for a handshake with his own hand outstretched in anticipation of shaking the hand of the father of rock 'n' roll. Chuck responded with an emotionless gaze, and after an interminable few seconds, the aborted non-event was over.

About fifteen years later, I was at a magazine photo shoot for St. Louis musicians, and Chuck was there in black suit coat and sporting his signature sailor cap. This time Chuck was amenable to signing a *Live in London* LP I had brought for the occasion. I knew better than to ask for a handshake . . .

BIG IN VEGAS

"Hey can we get your picture? Not her . . . just you," was the stranger's response after being informed that we were newly married and on a honeymoon, passing through Vegas.

How many times I've heard the expression "could have been a star." What's a star? Isn't "being a star" subjective? Being an *observer* seems paramount to me, and anonymity is priceless.

Maybe it's because I fell out of a moving car and landed on my head when I was five (the car door mechanism was frozen and there were no seat belts on a '65 Falcon), but perhaps this explains my quixotic chosen course of being an observer on a stage . . .

WILLIE NELSON

"**Y**ou just walked by Willie Nelson!"

"Huh? No way?"

"You just walked right past him in the parking lot."

This was about 1997 in Houston, Texas. Just as well to walk unobtrusively through the parking lot with Willie Nelson. It never seems fair to meet famous people anyway, as it's basically putting them on the spot. Willie has earned the respect of millions by shaking off adversity with sublime perseverance. He deserves to walk the parking lot in peace.

THE BEAR SUIT

An old friend and veteran of many tours of rock music duty going back to the early 1970s offered an anecdote of wisdom when he witnessed me struggling with finding the right balance of art and commerce in the 1990s.

I think this bit of passed-on wisdom helped set me on the correct path, so I'll offer it up here to anyone who may be thinking of entering into an artistic endeavor—be it art, music, poetry, film, or whatever the creative inspiration. I'll do my best to paraphrase Gary Schepers the way he tells the tale:

"I had a cousin who got a job playing trombone in the marching band at Disney World in Orlando, Florida. He was ambivalent about his job—on the one hand he felt lucky to be playing music, which he found to be good for his soul. Yet he had some existential reservations about the outward physical manifestations that went along with the job. Namely, donning a bear suit—which contradicted the music that felt so good for his soul."

Gary's cousin left this profound bit of wisdom to all the nascent artists of the world: "If you're gonna work at Disney World, sooner or later you're going to have to put on the bear suit . . ."

DISCOGRAPHY

• UNCLE TUPELO

No Depression (1990)

Still Feel Gone (1991)

March 16-20, 1992 (1992)

Anodyne (1993)

89/93: An Anthology (2002)

• SON VOLT

Trace (1995)

Straightaways (1997)

Wide Swing Tremolo (1998)

A Retrospective 1995-2000 (2005)

Okemah and The Melody of Riot (2005)

The Search (2007)

American Central Dust (2009)

• JAY FARRAR

Sebastopol (2001)

ThirdShiftGrottoSlack (EP) (2002)

Terroir Blues (2003)

The Slaughter Rule (2003)

Stone, Steel & Bright Lights (2004)

Live From Seattle (2004)

• OTHERS

Gob Iron – *Death Songs For the Living* (2006)

Jay Farrar and Ben Gibbard – *One Fast Move or I'm Gone* (2009)

Jay Farrar, Will Johnson, Anders Parker and Yim Yames – *New Multitudes* (2011)